Happy Birthday, Mike 8-28-92
With Love - from "Doc" + Norma Jean

Happy Birthday, Mike 8-28-92
With Love - from "Doc" + Norma Jean

Iowa
A Journey in the Promised Land

by

Kathy Aduddell Yoder

Quixote Press Publications

1991

Iowa

A Journey in the Promised Land

by

Kathy Aduddell Yoder

ISBN 1-878488-61-9

Published by

Quixote Press Publications
Fort Madison, IA

Camera-ready copy and layout by

PC Publishing
Vermillion, SD

Printed in the United States by

Pine Hill Press
Freeman, SD

To my two favorite Iowans

Dave and Ethan Yoder

and

to the people of Iowa
who invited me into their homes and their hearts.

Acknowledgments

My best friend, Dave Yoder, had to endure two pregnancies. After our son Ethan was born, he thought labor was over. When I started working on this book, he realized that it had only begun. With grace, friendship and love, he lived with me during both difficult times. Without him, this book would not have been born.

I am deeply indebted to many other people as well. Good ol' boy and publisher Bruce Carlson is a fun guy who never lost faith in me. He made this book possible.

Book designer and editor Pat Peterson used creativity, frankness and her wonderful sense of humor to make sure this book got on the right path and stayed there.

Photographer John Banasiak never runs out of ideas or patience. He was kind enough to share both with me.

John "Arlo" Wiggs' skill as a photographer is only matched by his skill as a friend.

A special thanks to Sue Roe, who always does the right thing and who is always my friend.

List of Photographs

Photo	Page
Dandelion Girls, southeast Iowa	2
Farmers and Tractors, southeast Iowa	3
Tomatoes Sunning, Laurel	4
Summer, Marshalltown	5
Ocheyedan	6
Near Colo	7
Southeast Iowa	8
Iowa River	9
The Road Home, central Iowa	10
Driving Across Iowa	12
Miller's Lunch, Le Mars	12
The Path, Cherokee County	13
Near Ocheyedan	14
Tree in Fog, central Iowa	15
Columbus Junction	16
Everly Brothers Drive, Shenandoah	17
One-way Church, Ft. Madison	18
Main Street, Hospers	20
Viking Queen, Hospers	20
Libertyville	21
Tama	21
Belle Plaine	22
Bait and Rec, Oakville	23
Alley Doors, Kalona	24
Stoplight, Shenandoah	26
Packwood	27
Bloomfield	27
Central Iowa	28
Centennial, Packwood	29
Barbershop, Fairfield	30
Bandshell, Hospers	32
Veteran, Marshalltown	33
Boy in Window, Marshalltown	34
Praying for Home, Fairfield	36
Moonies, Fairfield	37
Best Friends, Burlington	38
Merry-go-round, Des Moines	39
Central Iowa Fair, Marshalltown	40
Morgan, rural Marshalltown	42
Jefferson County	44

Photo	Page

First Day of School, Fairfield — 45
Green Castle, near Ferguson — 46
Iowa River — 47
Osceola County — 48
Silhouette of Corn — 49
Shimek Forest, Keosauqua — 50
Cat Web, rural Marshalltown — 51
Passionate Pigs, near Packwood — 52
George, southeast Iowa — 53
Grandpa's Girl, Marshalltown — 54
Lockridge Post Office, Lockridge — 56
Grandpa's Hat — 59
Window Shopper, Peterson — 60
Angel's Trumpet, southeast Iowa — 61
Mallory Cemetery, near Wapello — 62
Neighbors, Jefferson County — 64
Sowing Wild Oats, southeast Iowa, — 66
Near Marshalltown — 68
Tama — 69
Puppies 'N Boots, Des Moines — 70
Packwood — 72
Central Iowa Fair Rodeo — 73
Lily, Marshalltown — 74
Lunch Pail, Kalona — 75
Marshalltown — 76
Southeast Iowa — 77
The Spot, Marshalltown — 78
Fairfield — 79
Old School, near Kingston — 80
Hawkeye Church, rural Oakville — 80
Co-op Member, rural Battle Creek — 81
Hand of Cards, Fairfield — 82
In Passing, near Malvern — 83
Echoes, near Rubio — 84
Rainbow Bridge, Marshall County — 86
Dave, Ethan and Grandma Jo, Mediapolis — 87
Canadas, near Colo — 88
State Center — 89
Three Friends, southeast Iowa — 90

Preface

This book has been evolving for many years. It began with my experiences as a
child growing up in Ida Grove. My family lived one block from the edge of town.
From my bedroom window I could see cornfields. My grandparents, Lester and
Esther Aduddell, lived at the end of the block. Grandma paid my brothers, Mick
and Kim, and me ten cents a quart to pick her strawberries. Sometimes, Grandpa
and I snapped beans for her. Sometimes, she gave my brothers and me each a
cup of sugar for rhubarb dipping. My other grandparents, Delas and LaVerne
Lynch, lived on a farm near Battle Creek. We loved that farm. We played in the
barn, talked to the animals and ate Grandma's meals that were fit for threashers.

My parents, Duane and Shirley Aduddell, gave us a home filled with love and
laughter. We learned the value of hard work and simple pleasures. Going to the
Tip Top Cafe for a hot fudge sundae was a treat as wonderful to me then as win-
ning the Publisher's Clearing House Sweepstakes would be now.

I graduated from high school in Cherokee and from college in Cedar Falls,
worked as a photojournalist in Fairfield and Marshalltown and their surrounding
small communities.

No matter where I have traveled or what I have hoped for, I have found the
promised land right here, in the small towns, farms and cities of Iowa.

Now, I am a mother, and my hope is that my son will learn the values and ideals
that have guided me — that he will learn to love my Iowa.

Kathy Aduddell Yoder

Promised Land: a place or conditions believed to promise final
satisfaction or realization of hopes.

Webster's Collegiate Dictionary

Iowa's Child

I am a child of Iowa. My feet firmly planted in the land.
My toes sprout roots that dig deep in the black earth.
They branch out to join the network of brothers and sisters and mothers and fathers
    who have grown there before.

My crib is a cornfield. The sun warms me to sleep and the rain awakens me.
I feed on the black manna and grow with the corn.
I no longer bend and sway with the wind. I am tall and strong.
I pick up my child and carry him in my silken blanket until he takes root in the land
    and produces a child of his own.

I am a child of Iowa. I am born from the earth.
When I return, it will open up and cradle me again.
I will lie with my brothers and sisters and mothers and fathers.
My grandchildren and their children will take root,
    feet firmly planted in the land.

Spring:

Farmers walk differently in the spring. Straighter, more purposefully.

Women smile unconsciously as they hang their laundry outside for the first time.

And piglets, red-tailed hawks, colts, calves, and children all go a little crazy.

Summer:

Life slows way down after the Fourth.

Farmers walk with more effort when the primary activity of the day is watching for rain clouds in the west.

The future seems far away and not as important as sleeping on the porch and contemplating chirping crickets and the star-pregnant sky.

Autumn:

Life is quick. Farmers harvest. Squirrels store food. Birds gather and fly. Leaves fall. Children play hard. People work long. Their common goal: finish before first frost.

Winter:

The earth is wrapped in the quiet dignity of snow and cold. There's a clean, non-smell as children press their noses against frosted glass and listen for school closings on the radio.

And as the wind howls, book lovers curl up and read, and gardeners and farmers wistfully browse through seed catalogs over a hot cup of coffee—it won't be long now.

The Road Home

She had driven this road many times,
And, as always, when she hit the curve by the old apple tree,
    it was like greeting an old friend.
She knew where she was going and who she was.

Her pulse quickened and her head lightened.
She let out a sigh.
She was almost home.

She was eight years old,
    smelling her father's Old Spice aftershave,
    hearing her mother's homemade cherry pie bubble in the oven,
    watching her brothers play ball in the backyard.

It was her road.
The one that led home even though she didn't live there anymore.

A Spot in the Road

You've driven by it many times, but never stopped. Now you're hungry and you need gas, so you pull over.

You sit down in the red vinyl booth. A lady with a beehive calls you "honey" and flashes a motherly smile. You order comfort food: roast beef on white bread and mashed potatoes, all covered with gravy. You flip through the tabletop jukebox and punch in A-4, "Tennessee Waltz."

You lean back into the booth and relax while you eat. Outside, the cars pass by, the ones who never stop.

ONE WAY
SEVENTH DAY
ADVENTIST CHURCH

Small Town Directions

Ever try to get directions in a small town:

"Go to the only green house in town with a driveway. Turn right at the stoplight. Ya can't miss it. Only one in town. Go past Uncle Fred's house. Turn right at the old lumberyard. Ya know, the one that burnt down fifteen years ago.

Hang a left at Aunt Mill's place. Ya'll know it. She's the only one in town with a three-legged dog. He's friendly, though. Her dead husband sure wasn't. Old grump. 'Course, his porch light was a little dim, if ya know what I mean.

Take 'nother left at the ol' ball diamond. Played a few good games there, I tell ya. Go past the machine shop. One with the big dinersore out front. Jim Jahansen made it. Don't know what got in him. Guess after his wife ran off with that tellmarker he had to do sum'in to keep busy. I always said, 'Never trust teknology. Just ain't natural.'

Go right 'til ya git to a bumpy dirt road. Ifin' it's rainin', turn 'round. If not, take a left at the end and that's the place. Ol' Burley Buckster's house. Nobody's lived there comin' on thirty years. Hope ya like it. Was a beaut in its day. Hope ya move here. Sure could use a few more good talkers like you!"

Monuments

The Doughboy and the GI stand in the square where the old man sits. The Doughboy and the GI bear the names of the county's donations to war. They only used the first initials: P. Johnson, A. Jones. They were chiseled when the grief was fresh, the lesson painful, and everyone knew the names.

Now only the old man knows. The "P" was Peter, who showed him how to drive a team of Belgians when he was eight. "A" was Andrew, who stole his girl in high school.

Nobody remembers but him. Nobody remembers that his white hair was once red or that he earned medals in track. Nobody but him remembers how to translate the initials on the Doughboy and the GI.

The pigeons roost on the Doughboy and the GI. When it's lunch time, they fly down to the old man and he feeds them.

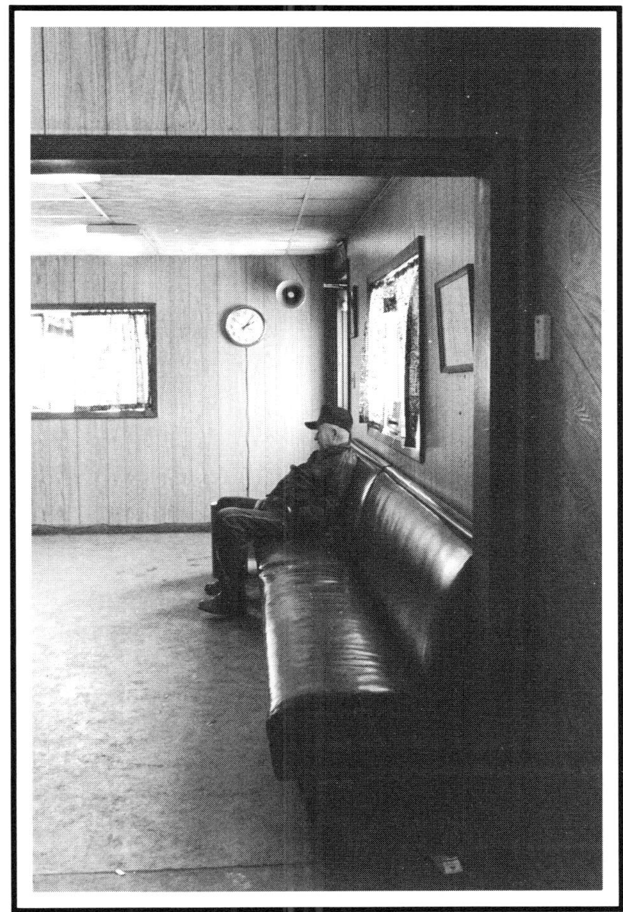

RAILWAY EXPRESS AGENCY
DRINK PEPSI-COLA
NevrNox ETHYL
HERRING HOTEL BELLE PLAINE
MANHATTAN GASOLINE
PHILLIPS 66 BATTERIES
VANO-TEX
AUTHORIZED STUDEBAKER SERVICE
QUAKER STATE MOTOR OIL
SAFETY SPARTON
CEDAR RAPIDS IOWA
Firestone
CHEW RED MAN TOBACCO
Firestone TIRE & BATTERY
SHELLANE BOTTLED GAS DISTRIBUTOR
DELCO
RED CROWN GASOLINE
BONE SCAL
SAVES THE MOTOR
DANGER 33,000 VOLTS ELECTRICITY
VITA-WAY LIVESTOCK
BLACK SATIN COAL
GOOD YEAR
SINCLAIR TIRES H-C GASOLINE
Wadhams Gasoline
AUTOLITE BATTERIES
KENDALL 2000 MILE OIL
BARNSDALL PRODUCTS
DERBY
Mobilgas
MERIT
ARBIE FEEDS
Try one More.
Golden Harvest
VOLTMASTER BATTERIES
STANDARD SERVICE
RED CROWN GASOLINE

PEPSI
Oakville Recreation
and Bait Shop
GROCERIES
TACKLE
OPEN 7 DAY WEEK

Cavity-Free

The alley by our house was one of my favorites. It was filled with treasures. One time I found an old lunch pail. It was white with a few flecks of red paint. I saw old Hank Wanders tottering down my alley and showed it to him.

"Don' touch that girl."
He never called me by name, at least not by my name.

"Don'cha know what's in there?"
I shook my head and my eyes grew big.

"There's germs in there."
"OOOOOH," I said, ready to be impressed.

"Don'cha know what germs is?"

He shifted from one bad leg to the other. Looked like he was on a teeter-totter.
I shook my head "no."

His teeth looked tiny and rotten. Gee, THAT'S what happens when you don't brush them. Instead of giving out suckers if you're good, the dentist should show you Hank Wanders. He could draw back a big curtain and say: "Come out here, Hank. We've got a little girl here who doesn't brush her teeth. Got anything to say to her?" And Hank'd just smile. And then you'd run home, probably screaming, and you'd brush. You'd brush those teeth so hard the enamel'd probably chip off. You'd brush them so much you'd glow in the dark.

"Germs can make you sick."
I stuck my head inside the pail, but I couldn't see anything.

Reading my mind, old Hank said, "You can't see 'em. They's invisible.
But they can make you real sick."

He teetered when he should have tottered and almost tipped over. But he regained his balance without missing a beat of his lecture. It was swelling up into a real good sermon, the kind that says: "I'm going to teach you something whether you want to learn it or not. I'm old. I've got the right. By God, I've got the calling."

And somehow, even though you're outside in a small town alley in Iowa, you hear the Mormon Tabernacle Choir singing, "HALLELUJAH! HALLELUJAH!"

"Don'cha ever play with things you don't know where they've been."

I would hear that same sentence over and over throughout my life. In fact, my epitaph will probably read: "She played with things she didn't know where they'd been."

And added in small letters at the bottom: "But she never had a cavity."

SENTINEL

Wednesday Night

Must be Wednesday night 'round 'bout 6:45, 'cause the front door of the Clairmaster house just opened. That house is a hundred years old and so's that squeak.

Here comes Lillian carryin' her green and yellow plastic lawn chair under one scrawny arm and her basket of knitting under the other. Neighborhood's been wonderin' if she's ever gonna finish that afghan for her daughter-in-law. Mabel down the street said Lillian figgers if she waits long enough, she can keep it for herself, the way those kids fight.

Lillian's settin' up her chair. Can tell her favorite spot in the backyard. The grass don't grow no more in her one sittin' area. She takes up her needles and starts knittin'. Won't be long now. 'Bout five minutes.

Nobody remembers when Lillian started her ritual. Seems like she was always doin' this. Sittin' in her backyard on Wednesday night, knittin' and waitin'.

7:00. Amtrak whirs by. Lillian lifts one needle and salutes. She smiles to herself. Another Wednesday night in the back yard.

Land of Boundary

Small towns hold the rural life in with neighborliness —
that come-over-for-a-cup-of-coffee-ness.

Jake Olsen calls his friend Mort Blake:

"Come on over, Mort. The wife's got coffee on and I think I smell
cinnamon rolls."

"I'll check on the hogs and be right there. And leave some rolls
for me. You're gettin' too fat."

"Yeah. Like you've seen your feet in the last ten years."

"I did. When the doctor took off that bunion."

"What? Oh, the Mrs. says to bring Marilu. She's got a new recipe and probably
some ol' gossip. Ouch! Don't poke me."

"Tell your wife to behave, Jake. See ya in five."

Visitors sometimes cross over into the town — strangers to friendly faces. And they are welcomed into the flock with open arms.

A young salesman stops at Pete Grenshaw's one-pump gas station:

> "Are ya sure you're not related to Henry Feltzer? Mavis, doesn't he look like he could be Henry's boy? Yep. Ya sure do. Better stay for supper. That tire can wait. It's not goin' anywhere. Na, it's no trouble. Gotta eat anyhow. Looks like you could stand a good home-cooked meal. Mavis is the best."

Barbed wire — metal — wood — electric fences all hold the animals in. The cattle, hogs, sheep. Sometimes they get out. But they usually come back, sometimes on their own, sometimes with a little help.

Young people in small towns leave. They go to glitzy places.

Melissa Janes talks to her high school friends over a Coke at Gleason's Cafe:

> "I can't wait to get outta this hole. I'm sick of talking to cows. I mean, REALLY, there's only one gas station in town. I'm goin' someplace big where no one knows me and my mom and dad and my grandpa and his grandpa. How B-O-R-I-N-G."

But they usually come back — on their own or with a little help.

And the next time they leave, they know the way back.

Growing Clothes

On the first day of school, Mary wore the new blue sailor dress.
She felt very grown up.
When she and her friends walked home, she filled the over-sized pockets with a red maple leaf,
    two sticks, some string and a giant marble with a lick of yellow in its center.
She believed her friends would be with her forever.

Her grandma made a stocking cap just for her.
But all the girls in her class teased her during recess.
"Only someone really dumb would wear a stocking cap like THAT," they taunted.
    They snatched it off her head and stomped it into the snow.
And as soon as she got home, she grabbed her Tony-the-Tiger pajama bag and spilled out her
    favorite pajamas, the ones with red bears and ribbing around the wrist and ankles.
She believed she was safe.

Her new Easter dress was egg-shell blue velveteen with pink roses at the collar.
    Her gloves were so crispy white she expected them to snap like cold carrots.
    Her pink bonnet had curly ribbons.
And when she looked in the mirror,
She believed the sun would always shine.

They dressed her in that scratchy black wool dress.
They said it was really no one's fault. How can two people die and there's no one to blame?
Her stomach really hurt.
If she could just get that awful dress off,
She believed she would understand.

Mary had grown big.
And when she overheard a good friend say unkind things about her,
    she went straight to the basement and pulled out her orange pajama bag.
The zipper still worked, and her favorite PJs were still inside.
But they no longer fit.
They had not grown with her.

Clothes should grow, but not grow up.
They'd never be too small for you.
You'd never be too big for them.

My Childhood Was Too Normal

Nobody I ever knew used drugs.
My biggest thrill was the tickly-tonge feeling I got from a Mr. Fizz tablet.

I never came home to an empty house.
The only key I carried was to a special box my dad made for my secret stuff.

My parents never divorced.
In fact, it was downright embarrassing the way they carried on.

The two biggest dilemmas at Halloween were
what to be and how much candy you could eat before you threw up.

The word "ulcer" was not in my vocabulary.
My main worry was that my mother would open my closet
    and find the living butterfly collection.

Our milk cartons had pictures of cows.

Maybe that's why when I wake up in the morning,
I'm humming before my feet touch the ground.

Best Friends

He stands up, bends over, ties his shoe. Well, tries to tie his shoe. Can't quite get the job done.

She climbs down from their log, leans over, finishes the task. Takes a sip of his pop.

"We used to be boyfriend-girlfriend," she says matter-of-factly.

She pops a bubble.

"Yeah, a long time ago. When we were young," he says.

He brushes a fly from her face.

"We were three."

She tickles him.

"Now we're just best friends."

He laughs and munches some of her Cheese Whizits.

"Yeah. Now we're four."

Their hands meet as they pet a scruffy alley cat.

"We're just best friends."

They run off, armed with water pistols.

The 'Lectric Chair

It was the kind of sunny day that warms you from the inside out. You feel like butter melting on toast.
A neighbor kid I called N.K. sat on the front porch with me.
From there we could see the whole world, but what held our attention was the catfish head someone had
nailed to the telephone pole in my front yard.

N.K. and I looked at it; talked about it; looked at it some more and said, "Ick, this is really gross."
We looked at it again. We wanted to stop, but we just couldn't.
Mr. Wizard covered that one time. So, it's pretty much a scientific fact: the ickier something is, the more
you have to look at it.

Flies buzzed around the head. "How many of them varmits do ya think there are?" asked N.K.,
who called any insect that name. I was the only one who knew his secret. He was terrified of bugs. Once,
when his big brother put a grasshopper down his shirt, he peed his pants.

"I don't know, two zillion million," I said.

"Nah. Five thousand hundred," he said.

We both laughed. Neither one of us was very good in math. That was NO secret.

A lineman came and climbed the telephone pole. He didn't see the catfish head.
He climbed from rung to rung as if he were just walking down the street. He stood at the top, leaned
back against his safety belt, pulled a phone from his pocket, made some twists and turns and talked.

"Seems like a long way to go just to make a phone call," N.K. whispered to me. We giggled.

The telephone man came down as easily as he'd gone up.
He smiled at us as if to say, "Thanks for watching the show," and left.

"Ya hafta be real careful 'round 'lectricity," N.K. announced sternly. "Like what goes through them up there."

"Why? What can happen?" I asked.

"You can die."

"No you can't," I said, refusing to believe.

"Really. Pinky swear. You can."

"Pinky Swear?" I asked as my eyes got bigger.
Pinky swear meant that we absolutely had to tell the truth no matter what.
It was a RULE we'd made up a long time ago.

"Yep," N.K. bobbed his head up and down. "Don'cha know 'bout the 'lectric chair?"

i shook my head from side to side.

"When people are really bad, they're taken to a room and tied to a chair. It's got 'lectricity in it.
Someone turns on the switch, and THEN THEY FRY."

We sat in a sort of stunned silence for a while.
Mr. Wizard had never talked about this.

I stood up to leave.

"Where ya goin'?" N.K. asked.

"In."

Suddenly the world had gotten too gross.

Bonanza

My girlfriends are in love with the color version of Little Joe.
But I love Hoss in black and white.
He's big and nice.
And somehow I know it's better to love your best friend
    than chase after an ideal.
Besides, the women who love Little Joe usually end up with his horse.

So, sprawled out on the floor, propped up by open palms
    supported by two skinny elbows,
I watch Hoss.

Of course, women who love the Cartwright men all end up dead.
    So, I rewrite the script.
Hoss and I ride off into the sunset,
And Little Joe is left feeding the horses.

Grandpa's Girl

We have a secret handshake
Me and my grandpa.
I hold out my nail-bitten hand.
His dirt-filled fingers take the offering.

He gets that twinkle in his eye.
I have one to match.
His thumb salutes mine.
He easily wrestles it down.

He wins.
He always wins.
And we laugh.
Me and my grandpa.

Our secret handshake complete

The last time I saw him
He took my hand and I took his.
His was shaky.
Mine was trembly.

I knew I could win/he knew I could win.
I saw it in his eyes,
But I didn't want the game to end.

He won.

Our secret handshake complete.

The Rummage Sale

Her husband laughed when she brought it home.
"It was only 50 cents," she said defensively.
"Fifty cents too much. What in the world are you gonna
DO with it?" he asked.

"Well, I don't know," she said, cradling the old toy barn and miniature
animals in her arms. "I guess I don't plan on DOING anything with it.
I just bought it because it makes me laugh."

"You are a strange woman, I always said," he teased.
"You have some deep, dark secret you wanna tell me?"

She was fiddling with the barn door. Opening and closing it.
Opening and closing it.

"One time when we were little, my older brothers and I visited some friends
on their farm. They had this huge, old barn, and the boys all climbed up this
ladder to the hay loft. But I guess my legs were too short, or I was scared or
something. Anyway, Joe and Bill wouldn't help me up, and from their
unreachable perch yelled 'Baby! Baby!' down at me. At first I was mad. They
were always leaving me outta the fun. But I got even. I kicked the ladder
down, pulled it out into the pig yard, calmly walked to the house, and didn't
say a word."

She smiles. "They weren't supposed to be up there. So when our friend's
father found them about three hours later, they really caught it."

"It was the last time they ever left me outta anything."

55

Grandma and Grandpa's Porch

My grandparents lived on a farm. Their house had a long front porch.
In fact, that porch was so long it seemed to wrap around the sides of the house,
    go back to where the chickens were,
        through the backyard gate,
            and into the big red barn where the cows lived.

Grandpa's chair sat on the porch.
    Countless times it saved me from those stupid chickens.
    They're supposed to be dumb,
        but they can smell fear as well as we can smell Kentucky Fried.
They smelled mine every single time I visited my grandparents,
    and they made my life a living hell
        until my grandma came out and shooed them away.

Chickens always gave Grandma respect.
    When my mom was little, she was terrorized by an old rooster.
        Every time he saw her, he chased her and pecked her.
Finally, my grandmother had had enough.
    She grabbed an old board, whirled it at that bird
        and served him up for supper.

After that, neither hens nor roosters messed with my grandmother.

But the best part about the long porch was that it made an excellent frame
    through which we could observe events.

The best show came one day
    when my brothers, my cousins and I were hastily corralled and herded indoors.
        We peered through the curtain that covered the picture window, across the porch
        and saw a sight we had not imagined.

A very large palomino in the front yard pasture was giving birth.
Of course, we didn't know exactly what was going on,
    but the panicked, hushed tones of the grown-ups behind us indicated
        it would be something really good.
We pressed forward until our noses became one with the glass.

I remember one of my cousins saying: "That's how babies are born."
        I didn't believe it for a minute.

Great-grandma and Blue-hair

Great-grandma lived in a small town in a stout house on a short street that led nowhere
except a cornfield.

Everybody knew her. She was squat and wide and wobbled when she walked.

Great-grandma and another blue-haired little old lady loved to sit on Great-grandma's porch in
their lawn chairs and talk. They talked while Great-grandma crocheted her doilies,
pillow toppings, tablecloths, furniture coverlets, doll dresses and anything else she fancied.
Great-grandma with her thick German accent, her friend with her small town twang,
gave advice to each other when they didn't want it — and to me all the time.

One day Great-grandma and Blue-hair decided to teach me to turn a cartwheel. For some
reason, they thought my time had come. They sat on their lawnchair-thrones, unable to cross
their legs, knees wrapped in Ace bandages, smelling of Ben-Gay and started their instruction
with the certainty of Olympic coaches.

"No, no, Ka-ty (pronounced Kathy without the "h"). Not right." And, as she had always done,
Great-grandma placed her right index finger on top of her left index finger and created that
peeling-a-carrot motion, which in younger years had been accompanied by "shame, shame."

Blue-hair said something I couldn't hear and the two laughed and laughed until they looked
like young girls sharing a boy-secret. This did not give me confidence in my performance.

Blue-hair said something about this being "better than the Ed Sullivan Show."

After an especially ungraceful attempt, I looked up at Great-grandma and Blue-hair. They were
laughing so hard I thought they might fall off their lawn chairs, roll down the porch steps and
somersault into the grass.

I never learned how to turn a cartwheel.

The Carpenter's Hat

It hangs on the wall waiting for the man to come and wash his face in the back
porch basin and kiss the wife. She is waiting, too.

He combs his hair, straining to see in the cracked and silver-spotted dime store
mirror. She hung it there years ago. She knew he liked the way he looked.

He takes his hammer out of its loop, empties his nail-filled pockets and
changes into a clean pair of overalls. Can never have too many.
"Darn college kids wear 'em now. Drove the price up."

Supper is cooking on the stove — corn-on-the-cob boiling in a huge pot; gravy bub-
bling in the black iron pan. He grabs his can of tobacco, puts on the hat and stops
outside by the fruit cellar door to roll a cigarette. "Air smells good."

The garden's 'round back. "It looks good. Well, good enough.
Too many weeds." He raises his cane but misses his mark.
"Damn rabbits, when did they get so fast?"
Almost tips over. His hat slips a little.

It never falls off. Just stays perched on his head like crows on a telephone wire.
The rabbits never leave. Even when confronted by three boys and two BB guns,
death-thoughts make them cackle.

He bought the hat back in the thirties, when times were hard, but he looked good.
Got his woman, didn't he? He built a house and they built a family.
The kids grew up straight as studs and strong as two-by-fours.
Now they do the building.

"Just me and the woman."

Indoors he puts the hat on its hook, washes up for supper in the back porch basin
and looks again in the mirror. Oh, the pretty heads he used to turn.

He sits at the table in his captain's chair and waits for supper.

Window-Shopper

She sits in her favorite chair and traces its familiar arms with her hands.
They are like the arms that once cradled her, the strong arms of her man.

That was long ago when he was goofy-young and horse-healthy-strong;
She was wrinkle-free and too silly-sweet to worry;
their love made the rules.

He moved the earth. She harvested a family.
When another season passed, they began again.
She thought it would never change.

There wasn't much money.
She had her hens. He had his wood.
She took her egg money and bought him a pocket knife.
He took his wood and carved her a chair.

"When do I have time to sit in a chair?" she laughed.
"Some day," he said.

Now she has the time. Time to sit. Time to rock.
Time to think. Time to draw back the crinkle of years to window-shop.
Her lace-curtained face and the face-wrinkled window whir and blur
until she makes out a figure.
Her man.

Like a grocery list, she says, "I'll take that one and put him on our old piece of land.
Throw in my children 40 years ago. Don't forget my hens."

She pauses.
"And I'll take some new curtains. These are too old."

The Color TV

He bought the color TV the day after she died. It seemed odd, since their lives had been black and white. Maybe it was his way of coping with grief. But more likely he was tired of her scripts. Either way, the day after the funeral, he got his favorite chair from the basement, brought out a TV tray, took his TV dinner out of the oven and sat down in front of the new set with a fork in his hand and a smile on his face.

The TV sat smack dab in the center of the livingroom. She would never have allowed this interruption of the traffic pattern. Her rooms were orchestrated for practical purposes. In truth, she probably would have been more upset with him for this afront to symmetry than for having an affair. And the thought of him in her kitchen would have killed her quicker than the heart attack.

His first venture in THERE had been to get a glass of water. He had felt a sense of freedom, kinda giddy. He had opened a cupboard and looked in, and with a sense of abandon, he had thrown out cans and cans of tuna. Every Tuesday for 45 years, they had eaten tuna casserole for supper. No more.

It was then he thought of frozen dinners. Never in his life had he eaten one. "It's just not natural, eating a meal in a box," she always said. He had immediately turned around, grabbed the keys and headed for the store.

Twenty-five. He bought twenty-five frozen dinners.

But cooking was another matter altogether. He had run a large business, but he didn't know how to run an oven. He left the TV dinner in the oven too long—the peas stuck to the aluminum foil and the apple crisp was the color of tar. It smelled a little odd, but to him it was as splendid as those fancy meals they fix on those cooking shows on PBS.

So, he sat in his chair with his feet up on the ottoman and the TV blaring.

"Tomorrow," he thought. "Tomorrow, I'll get some of that store-bought cookie dough. Tomorrow," he giggled, "I'll BAKE."

Food

Iowa hospitality is thicker than mosquitoes on the Fourth of July and always involves food.
Good food.
Iowa home cookin' sticks to your ribs like your old aunt's lips on your five-year-old cheek.
     No matter how hard you try to pry it loose, it sticks.
Food is an important part of life. You grow food. You eat food. You feed food.
     And, if you're not careful around the hog lot, you are food.

You eat breakfast in the morning, dinner at noon and supper at night.
Of course, a friend might stop over "to coffee" mid-morning or mid-afternoon.
This means you: a) make a pot of coffee, b) eat something sweet, c) sit in the kitchen and d) laugh a lot.

If friends come over after supper for a friendly game of 500, the host wife will serve a "little lunch"
     afterwards, around 9 or 10 o'clock.
The lunch includes good coffee and/or sun tea if it's summer, sandwiches on buttered white bread,
     maybe one of the many thousands of Jello salads made in Iowa,
     and some very rich, very delicious, very fattening dessert.

If the guest wife says she's on a diet, the response is always a friendly, but firm,
     "Oh, you can start tomorrow. A little bit won't hurt."
The host wife says this as she plops a 2,000-calorie temptation in front of the guest wife,
     arms her with a fork and watches her like a hawk until she takes that first bite,
     at which time the host wife knows the guest wife is a goner.

And if the guest husband thinks he's going to get by with just one piece of dessert, he's wrong.
The host wife knows how to cajole and persuade just enough to make the guest husband take that second
     piece of pie or cake or whipped cream delight and not feel guilty.
In fact, the guest husband ends up convinced he has performed some patriotic duty.

At the end of the evening when the guest couple goes home,
     the guest wife won't know if it's that second piece of pie that pops the guest husband's buttons
     or just plain pride.

To Town

They said they moved to town because the tractors didn't run themselves and the combines didn't harvest the corn. The hens gave no eggs. The cows no calves. The pigs lost their oink.

And Grandpa is happy.

Each morning, he and men like him hold important meetings at the cafe and wear uniforms: bib overalls and seed corn hats. Over dozens of doughnuts and gallons of coffee, they solve the world's problems and predict rain. When someone's ache is accurate, he is lifted up in the pecking order until a bunion forecasts better. If someone stretches the truth, the others pretend not to notice. They take turns
telling their stories.

Grandpa goes home, wearing a smile, and writes her a note.
"I told them that story you said you never wanted to hear again. They loved it."

And Grandma is happy.

She goes to the Senior Citizens Center and learns to samba with other grandmas. Somewhere in between the two-step and the waltz, they compare grandchildren photos and daughter-in-law stories.

The grandma with the worst daughter-in-law is lifted up and held in great esteem until another knocks her down with a story about naughty grandchildren. They make crafts and sell them. They make everything you could never imagine you would ever want or need.

Grandma goes home, takes her earnings from Bingo or the toilet paper doll and places them on the kitchen table. In a shaky hand she writes, "Grandpa, tomorrow's coffee's on me."

And Grandpa is happy.

GOODYEAR
7.50-16LT
TUBELESS

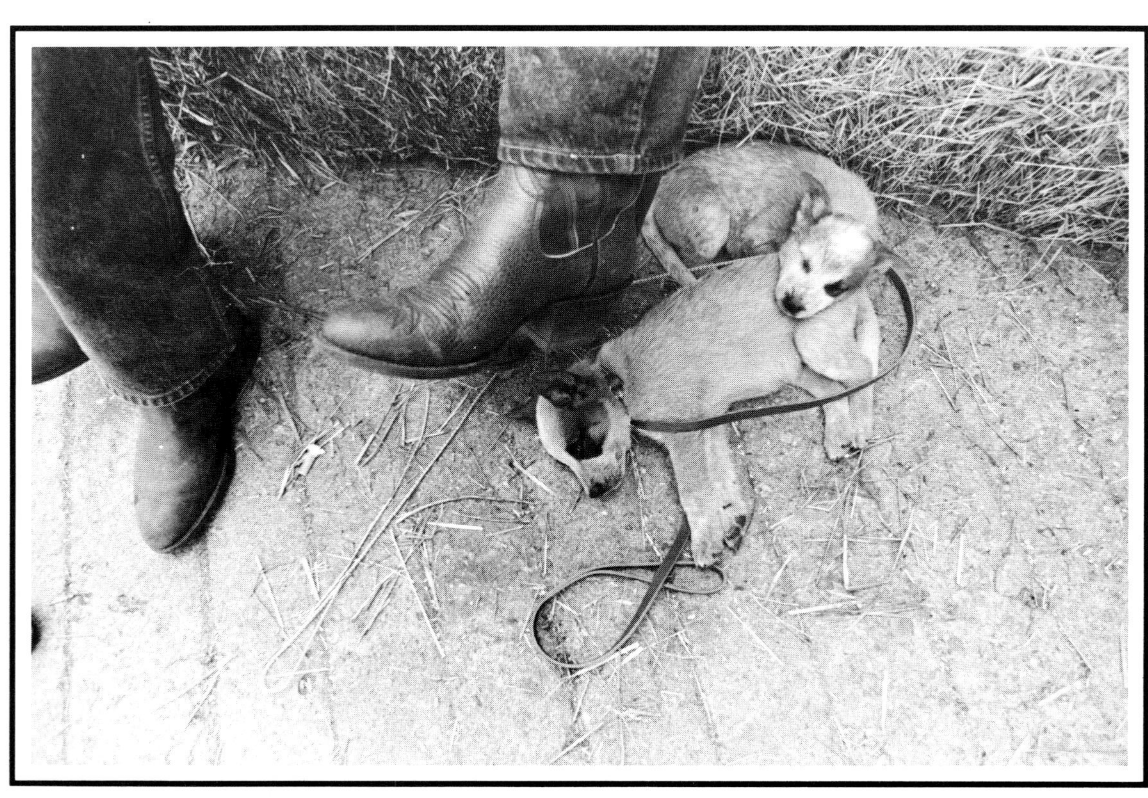

Boots

She had driven all night to get there.
Now, as she hurried through the front doors,
she forgot to prepare herself for that hideous antiseptic smell.
God, how she hated it.
Made her want to puke every time she inhaled.

And the light.
Why were hospitals lit up like interrogation rooms?
It wasn't just the brightness.
Some kinda glare made her eyes wiggle.

If that wasn't enough to drive her crazy, the lack of color pushed her
over the edge. Everything and everyone was white.
And everyone wore those rubber soled shoes.
You can never hear them coming.
They just appear, like ghosts with bad taste in footwear.

She turned the corner and found the information desk.
Yes, she was immediate family.
Down the hall, two rights and a left, then three-quarters of the way
on the right side, room 404.

She followed the directions.
After she turned left, she stopped.
She looked down the long corridor, and knew which room was his.
Outside his door sat his old work boots.

The original color was long gone.
The laces were chewed. Mud stuck to the sides.
She smiled. He must have left them there to guide her.
Even now, he thought of everyone else.

The Cowboy

He watched his favorite western on TV. He was an old man, but not too old to enjoy something new. He sat in his chair. Over the years it had worn in all the right places and had molded to his form. No one else ever sat in it. It waited for him to take his place. And they became one, like a cowboy and his horse.

He was the kind of skinny that leads to a robbery. Old age was stealing his life. Eventually, he'd be so skinny he'd just disappear.

But tonight he was strong. Tonight he was in control. From his lofty steed he battled the bad guys, winked at the pretty girls and ran a cattle ranch. Tonight, time was not a buzzard circling its prey and waiting for a free lunch. As he reined in his mount, he laughed. He liked being the great cowboy.

The one, always in the forefront, laughing and joking,
   sometimes wore a hat made from beer cans.

The other, in the background, shyly smiling,
   always wore petite pearl earrings, even in the garden.

They had always been friends.

THE SPOT
COCKTAILS
FOOTLONGS
89¢

HOME OF
A HOG RAISING
CO OP
MEMBER

Mouse Man

He had worked at the newspaper 40 years, from the days of hot lead type to ticker tape to computers. He was the only person in the office who always knew the difference between "affect" and "effect."

The only time he had ever missed work was when he served in WW II. In his uniform he was a good-looking young man with a straight back and eyes full of dreams, before the years of crouching in a corner rustling newspaper pages and caring for a sick mother nibbled away at him.

A young woman at work collected lost animals and shy people. One Christmas she just showed up at his house with a plate of red and green Jello cookies. He was so surprised he could barely move, but accepted the gift from a safe corner behind the door of his enclosed porch. Every corner of the room was piled high with stuff. She saw it as a nest made of his favorite things.

No one knew what he did after he left work. Someone said he liked organs and drove out of town for recitals. She would imagine him after a long day hunched over in his corner, scurrying home, scuttling through stacks of papers and mail and books and sitting down in his sagging recliner. She could see him turning on some soothing organ music, kicking off his shoes, snuggling down and being hugged by that chair.

And on that Christmas morning when she took him Jello cookies, she imagined him in that chair, munching cookies and smiling, as crumbs fell.

Echoes

As he wanders through his mind,
time and time again he stumbles over the same memory.
He doesn't know if it is important
or if his brain is just stuttering.

He's a little boy with two cowlicks and four hundred freckles.
His three brothers and four sisters aren't born yet.

His mother is hanging out laundry—it slaps in the breeze.
His father is driving a team of Percherons—they whinny and grunt.

He climbs onto his furry roan.
He uses his feet to make the horse "go!"
The four glass coasters squeak on the wet grass.
Boy and horse fly down the long hill—his mother drops the laundry—
his father stops plowing.
They meet at the bottom of the hill.
They gather him in their arms, waiting anxiously for him to speak.

"Do it again!" he giggles.

Every Saturday night at 6:00, Dave, Ethan and I watch "Star Trek: The Next Generation." I'm fascinated with life in the future. As a child, I waited for my copy of "My Weekly Reader" with the anticipation of a gourmand waiting for a feast. I devoured issues about video phones and satellite stations on Mars.

I spend a lot of time thinking about the future. I have a really big wish list: 1) end racism; 2) cure disease; 3) stop war; 4) eradicate poverty.

But when I close my eyes, my hopes become more defined — simpler —

like

having a long life with my husband
a good and healthy life for my son
and
manning a satellite station on Mars.

Promised Land

They were of this land.
    They lived off the bounty of this land —
        The Indian farmers — the Ioway.
    Their maize, beans and squash flourished
        in the fertile soil;
    Their families grew and prospered
        along the lush banks of its rivers.
    They buried their dead in this sacred land.
    The promise fulfilled.

White men came —
    Trappers, explorers and traders —
    And saw the promise of this land.
    Their businesses profited from the fruits of this land,
    And they returned east with their trade boats filled
    And stories of the great land between two rivers.

More European descendents and immigrants came —
        Norwegian, German, Irish, Swede —
    All made new homes in this land.
    Their crops prospered in the rich soil.
    Their families grew along the banks of the Little Sioux,
        the Skunk, the Nishnabotna, the Iowa.
    They buried their dead in this sacred land.
    The promise fulfilled.

They still come —
        Laotian, Latino, Soviet Jew —
    Filled with hopes of prosperity;
    Building new families with new dreams.
    Eventually, they too will bury their dead in the sacred land.
    The promise fulfilled.